My ALABASTER BOX

My ALABASTER BOX

Inspirational Poems for the Heart and Soul

DORIS COLLIER

Higgins
Publishing

Oakland, CA

REFERENCE: RICK WARREN -"THE PURPOSE DRIVEN LIFE"
WELL DONE MY CHILD
IT'S NOT ABOUT ME
PURPOSE
GOD SMILES
WHO AM I
I'M NOT AN ACCIDENT

T.D. JAKES - SERMON
DRY PLACE

Higgins Publishing books may be purchased for educational, business, or sales
promotional use. For more information email: specialmarkets@higginspublishing.com

HARDBACK EDITION

Library of Congress Control Number: 2013935543

Collier, Doris

My Alabaster Box : inspirational poems for the heart and soul / Doris Collier

ISBN 978-1-941580-29-5 (HB)

Higgins Publishing, its Logos and Marks are service marks of Higgins Publishing.

Publisher: Higgins Publishing
            http://www.higginspublishing.com

Cover Design by: Higgins Publishing
Front Cover Illustration by: Keven Winston
Back Cover Photograph by: Glamour Shots
Edited by: Dora Woodard

Dedication

I dedicate this book to my parents both deceased.
Because of the love and strength that they instilled in me
I have been able to walk through many adversities
and still hold on to their teaching by example
to love unconditionally and forgive as I would want to be!

I want to thank my Pastors, Joel and AnnaLisa Jones
for their obedience in hearing and obeying the voice of God
to bring this project to fruition, and my grandson
Keven Winston for using the gift God gave him
to create such a beautiful cover.

I thank Dora Woodard for taking time out of her life
to read all the poems and provide lists of scriptures that
were suitable for every poem!

TO GOD BE THE GLORY!!!

CONTENTS

FOREWORD
Pastors Joel & AnnaLisa Jones

~

Greetings, and welcome to Doris Collier's book release entitled "My Alabaster Box." Sister Doris has been blessing many people throughout the years with her wonderfully anointed poems. My wife and I have personally been touched weekly by her divine gift, as our church recently discovered that God miraculously sends Doris messages through her poetry that confirm the themes of the sermons for our weekly service. So accurate are her poems, that Doris now blesses our congregation with a poetic message just prior to my weekly sermons. In that sense, we like to think of her poems as very tasty and nutritious appetizers just prior to the entree. However...we're certain that readers will come away satisfied and satiated, finding that these poems will more than aptly satisfy their spiritual taste buds, all on their own - Bon appetite.

Pastors Joel & AnnaLisa Jones
Spirit of Truth Church Worldwide

INTRODUCTION

I was born September 18, 1950 in Lawton Oklahoma, to Joe and Aline Collier, the third of 3 girls. We moved to Wichita Kansas when I was 3 years old at which time 6 more siblings came along. I remained in Wichita until 1984 when I, along with my 4 children relocated to Sacramento California. A state that I said I would never live in, but God had a plan! I left Wichita with $100.00 and when I arrived in Sacramento, with only my son at the time, I had $10.00 left! After being unsuccessful at finding a job in Sacramento, I moved to Oakland California in 1985.

I grew up in a loving household where my parents showed us by example how to give unconditional love and forgiveness! In our house church was not an option, it was a part of life! Even though, like most small children, I wasn't really paying attention God was planting His Word in my spirit!

At a time in 2004 when there was much turmoil in my life, the Holy Spirit began to give me words that helped me to stand! As I began to share the poems with others they too were encouraged. The poems were coming so frequent that I had to keep paper and pencil on me at all time, or near my bed.

I was on an airplane coming from Kansas sitting comfortably in an isle seat and hoping that no one sat next to me. Just as I had that thought a very tall man with a very deep voice walked up and asked if anyone was sitting next to me, I told him no and he sat.

He noticed the book that I was reading "Breath Prayers" and said that he was just reading from the book of Timothy. I told him about the poems and how they were coming and that I didn't know what God wanted me to do with them. He immediately said "put them on bookmarks" and I did!

I have long had the desire to publish the poems at the urging of my family and friends. The title "My Alabaster Box" came after hearing someone sing that song and stating that they believed our Alabaster Boxes are our hearts and the issues that flow from our hearts! And I now share with you "My Alabaster Box."

I
PRAISE

MY ALABASTER BOX

I have an Alabaster Box
given to me in perfect condition,
I allowed it to be tarnished
as I struggled with my life's mission.

I stored in this box
sin, hurt, fear,
disappointment & pain.
All of these caused my
Alabaster Box to be stained!

But my Father is so good,
so loving and forgiving.
He forgave me my sins,
showed me the true meaning
of living!

From my Alabaster Box now flow
the lessons of my life!
No longer do I allow the
things that caused me strife!

My Alabaster Box once again
is like new! The words that follow
the Holy Spirit gave me to see
me through, and I can now
share the content of
My Alabaster Box
with you!

Ezekiel 36:26

GLORY OF GOD

Everything wears the glory of God. All creation
reflects His Light. The sun by day and the moon
and stars by night.

All things give Him praise, even the rocks and
the trees. His glory is on every good thing all
that our eyes can see.

Open your eyes and see the glory of God!

Psalm 29

GLORY TO YOUR NAME

My Soul has reconnected with this
Spirit inside of me. Reconnected with
You my Creator and You have opened
my eyes to see.

I've been given just a glimpse of Your
power and Your grace! One day I know
I will see You face to face!

Then I will understand why You love
me so! Why despite my sinful ways
Lord, You never let me go!

I don't have words to express the
feelings deep inside of me! How do
I say "Thank You" for saving and
setting my spirit free?

So, I say "Glory, Glory, Glory to
Your name!

The little glimpse You have shown
me is almost more than I can bear!
It's beyond my comprehension that
there is so much more of You there!

You are my Redeemer, my Comforter,
my Savior and my Friend! You are my
Healer and my Provider! Please stay
with me to the end!

Glory, Glory, Glory to Your name!

2 Samuel 22:49-51

I MUST PRAISE

You have loved me beyond my understanding and
supplied my every need! Your mercy is all over me
yet Your word I struggle to heed!

You have made me just a little lower than Yourself
and shared Your awesome power with me. You have
given me the gift of sight so that more of You I am
able to see.

With all that I am I must praise You and glorify Your
name! Be an example to those around me so that
they will do the same!

I have prayed and You have answered, giving protection,
healing and grace! Not holding back any good thing always
willing to forgive my mistakes

My flesh is so weak ever slipping into sin. Yet Your
compassion and unfailing love is always there welcoming
me back in.

Who am I that You never turn away that You love me so.
No matter how deep in sin I sink You never let me go!

With all that I am I must praise You! When I think about
All that You have done, the Father of all creation, the
Great I AM that I Am, the Majestic and Holy One!

I Must Praise!

Psalm 9:1-2

TOUCHED BY GOD'S HAND

I've been given a gift, a gift
from above!
A miracle of healing for someone
I love!

The devil attacked and meant
her harm!
But God sent the Holy Spirit
to wrap her in His arms!

What an awesome experience to be
touched by God's love!
What a wonderful testimony to claim
healing from above!

God said by the stripes of
Jesus Christ we are healed!
I am a living witness,
that promise is real!

I give God all the Glory!
Honor and Praise!
Every chance I get holy
hands I will raise!

The gift will be used to help
others who suffer,
to assure them God's there
with healing to offer.

When the doctors are puzzled,
and don't understand,
we will look at them, smile
and say,
"She's been touched by God's Hand!"

Isaiah 53:5

II
MAJESTY

JESUS, THE GIFT THAT KEEPS ON GIVING

God gave Himself as the Holy Spirit to a virgin girl named Mary.
He sent an angel to let her know of the Gift that she would carry!

He poured Himself into a man and called Himself His Son!
He came to earth as a sacrifice for the redemption of
everyone!

A Gift to mankind that keeps on giving!
The word of God, the Water that is living!

The Rose of Sharon, the great I Am that I Am, the Bright
and Morning Star! Jesus the Messiah, what a gift You are!

When the Gift fulfilled His earthly mission and had to go away, He
sent yet another Gift, the same Holy Spirit that filled Mary that day!

The Holy Spirit came bearing more gifts for us to possess. Gifts
that help us to grow and make it through
our earthly test!

The gift of prophesy, wisdom, knowledge,
discernment and tongues. Interpretation, faith, healing
and miracles available to everyone!

The Holy Spirit also came bearing fruit: love,
joy, patience, kindness, goodness, all fruit that we must share!
Faithfulness, gentleness and self-control, no matter how much you
consume them there is always more there!

The Gift that keeps on giving will never go away!
All we need do is accept the Gift, use the Gift and share the Gift
every day!

Jesus is the Gift that keeps on giving,
He is the Word of God, and the
Water that is living!

LIFE

Life! Is it just a word? Is it a situation?
or maybe a circumstance! Life! Is it
some kind of magical dance?

Or is it a precious gift from God born out of
love, mercy and grace? Is it what God
uses to take our spirits to a higher place?

Life! It is the breath of God! If we don't
acknowledge that breath, life is just a
word, just a situation, just a circumstance!

Life Is The Breath of God!

MARY'S BABY

"In the beginning was the Word, and the Word was with God, and
the Word was God. He was with God in the beginning"
John 1: 1, 2

When man could not stand under the temptation of Satan and
ushered sin into the earth, the Word stepped forward and offered
Himself so that man could have a new birth.

He knew that His Father was too Holy to ever look on sin.
So He said "I'll go down and redeem man so that My Father can
look again!"

He came through the womb of a woman, the Holy Spirit
placed Him there, to bear the weight of all sin, to show how much
He cared.

He came as the image of God, for all mankind to see!
The image of God's greatness and His majesty!

For every sin that we can possibly imagine Mary's Baby
came to set us free! For every liar, murderer, child molester and
thief, He willingly let them put nails in His feet!

Mary's Baby stretched out His arms and let them nail Him to the
cross, so that sinful man would be redeemed,
so our souls would not be lost!

A crown of thorns they placed on His head then pierced Him in His
side trying to make sure He was dead!

The blood and water that flowed from His side
contained power
beyond our comprehension!
One drop is worth more than all
silver and gold, or anything else that we can mention!

What they didn't know is that He **gave** Himself! Nothing they did would
have hurt Him! He could have come down from that cross leaving
mankind forsaken!

For us Mary's Baby willingly paid the price! He was beaten beyond
recognition, bruised for our iniquities,
scorned and crucified!

Mary's Baby volunteered to step down from
His heavenly throne to make all things new! Jesus,
the "Great I Am" gave His mortal life
for sinners like me and you!

Isaiah 53:5-6

POWER IN THE NAME

There is power in the name of Jesus!
Power beyond compare.
Power in the name of Jesus, take your cares
to Him and leave them there.

Jesus, Messiah, Savior is His name! yesterday, today
and forever He is the same.

There is power in the name of Jesus.
Power we can't understand.
Power in the Name of Jesus, call Him, reach out
and take His Hand!

Philippians 2:9-11

THE BREATH OF GOD

God is so awesome just think about what He has done.
He spoke a word and created life, the earth, moon and sun.

He placed the stars across the sky, created planets far
away! Creatures of every kind He created on the 5th
and 6th day.

He made a man by forming clay! Breathed life into
his spirit. He gave this man charge over all the earth,
and a mate with which to share it!

He gave this man all he would need, just asked him
one thing not to do! Because man went against God's
will, sin was passed down to me and you!

But God is so awesome and He loves us so much, that
He Himself came down! He made a sacrifice for us, and
turned that sin around!

Why would you not want to please Him after all that
He has done? He only wants the best for us, that is
why He gave His Son!

Think about your life today! And every time You breathe,
remember, that is the breath of God in you! The
magnitude of its power we cannot truly conceive!

God breathed into us some of His awesomeness! We
should strive to let it show! He's coming back to
reclaim that breath, the day you will not know!

So, live your life honoring God in every way! Live your
life as though you know Jesus is coming back today

Genesis 1:1; Genesis 2:7

What A Love

An angel was sent with a message to a virgin girl!
A message of the Messiah who would be born to save
the world.

He shed some of His power and His majesty so that Mary's
womb could contain Him, so that we could be set free.

He stepped down from His throne and took off His Kingly
robe. He wrapped Himself in our earthly flesh so that
we could be made whole!

What A Love!

A baby, born in a manger and wrapped in swaddling
clothes. Born to die, no greater love has ever been shown!

He came to start as we did so that our struggle He would
know. He humbled Himself for us because He loves us so.

What A Love!

He walked this earth becoming sin, knew that He would
suffer. For us He did this! That kind of love could come
from no other!

Our minds cannot comprehend the magnitude of the love
He has shown. A love that is wider, longer, higher and
deeper than anything we know!

What A Love!

He stepped down from His throne to come and see about
us! And all He asks in return is that we love Him and
that in Him we put our trust!

Love thy neighbor as thy self, He also told us to do! And
forgive them as I have forgiven you!

Jesus the Messiah, the Hope for all mankind, Jesus the
Lamb of God came to bear your sin and mine!
Oh! What A Love!

III
GRATITUDE

Amazing Grace

I'm forever grateful Lord, that You didn't
wait for me! You came and snatched me
from a life full of misery!

I'm forever grateful that You hung on the
cross. That You gave Your life to save
my soul, a soul that was lost.

I' m forever grateful that You opened my
eyes to see, that the life I thought I
controlled was actually my destiny.

A destiny that You planned the beginning
and the end You know. The in-between
has all the lessons that cause my spirit
to grow.

I' m forever grateful for each obstacle that
I face. I'll make it through each one because
of Your Amazing Grace!

"I'm Forever Grateful!"

I Peter 2:9-10

DEW FROM HEAVEN

Thank You for the dew drops! Fresh
and pure each day. Appearing as
droplets of tears as You pour out
Your mercy and grace!

The overflow of Your love like dew
drops in the morning fall! Refreshing
our spirits and proclaiming You Lord
of all!

Thank You for the dew drops that
nourish and feed the earth! A
redeeming of life, just like our
Savior's birth!

Proverbs 3:19,20

How Do You Explain?

How do you explain God the Creator of all there is. How do you
explain Him that died while He yet lived.

How do you explain God as that Something that stirs within. He's
Alpha and Omega, the beginning and the end.

How do you explain God who put everything in its proper place,
whose presence is so holy no one can look upon His face.

How do you explain God who commanded time to begin, who with
that same authority will bring time to an end.

He's larger then we will ever know or be able to understand. How
do you explain God who holds the world in His hands.

He poured Himself into a man and came to earth to die, through the
womb of a woman He did this while He yet remained on high.

How do you explain God who is everywhere always. How do you
explain that He was here before the beginning of days.

How do you explain He that can tell sickness and disease to go
away. How do you explain God who tells the winds not to blow the
rivers not to flow and they obey!

How do you explain that He is three in one, the Father the Holy
Ghost and also the Son.

There is no explanation for Someone so great. No words can
explain Him it's all about our faith!

LORD YOU HAVE BLESSED ME

Lord You have blessed me beyond
my comprehension.
You have blessed me in ways too
numerous for me to mention.

You have blessed me with every
good and perfect thing in my life!
You have blessed me Lord in
the middle of strife.

I thank You and I give You
praise, every chance I get
holy hands I will raise!

How can I repay You for all
that You do?
Show me Father, what I
can do for You!
Because...

Lord You Have Blessed Me!

No Complaint

How can I moan?
How can I complain?
When You have done so much
for me, when Your love has
never changed.

When worry overtakes my mind,
prompt me to stop and pray.
Pray with the assurance that
You will take all worry away.

Holding on the many
promises in Your Word,
I cannot let the things of this
world cause me to be disturbed!

Isaiah 26:3

Out of Control

I am out of control! I have lost my mind!
The same thoughts consume me all the time!

I have the same thoughts every day! No matter
how I try they won't go away!

If anybody asks you what's the matter with me
just tell them I'm out of control because my
spirit has been set free!

Free to sing and dance, to worship and praise!
Free so that no matter where I am holy hands
I can raise.

When I think about His goodness and all He has
done for me, how can I not be out of control when
He has set me free!

I prayed, He answered! I cried He dried my tears!
I moaned and He turned it into a song! I was afraid
and He took away my fears!

I am out of control and it feels so good!

Psalm 40:1-3

THANK YOU

Thank You Lord for humbling me.
For bringing me to my knees!
Help me not to think so high that
I can't see what You want me to see!

Thank You Lord for humbling me!
So that I can hear Your voice.
That voice that when I listen always
leads me to the right choice.

Thank You Lord for loving me
In spite of my sin! For giving me all
I need and for calling me Your friend!

Thank You Lord!

IV
PURPOSE

HOLY PLACE

There is a Holy Place inside of me!
A place that when I was lost I couldn't be!

This place is quiet, peaceful and calm.
There I meet Jesus, He holds me in His arms!

He talks to me in this Holy Place and allows me
to rest. He offers me forgiveness as my sins
I confess!

There is a Holy Place inside of me! It's a place
of worship and serenity!

In this Holy Place my spirit is set free! It's a
place reserved for Jesus & me!

I love that Holy Place inside of me!

Psalm 91:1

I THIRST

I thirst for the Living Water! So that I will thirst no
more!
I thirst for You Jesus, You I worship and adore!

I thirst for the Living Water! That Water that sets me
free.

Free to do what You would have me do, to be all that I
have
been anointed to be!

As a deer pants for the water, my heart pants for You.
The Living Water Christ Jesus, who made all things
new!

I thirst for You Jesus!

Psalm 42:1-2

LAND BETWEEN

Carry me Lord in the land between. The land where my
Spirit is weak! Gird up my legs, renew my strength as
Your face I seek.

I give up my will as I step into Yours, knowing provision
You will make! The land between, a time for growth
with every step I take.

A time for prayer, a time for praise, for transformation
and faith renewed! Thank You for the land between
as I draw closer to You!

Romans 8:26-28

LIVE IN ME

Live in me Jesus! Let Your love show
through me! Live in me Jesus!
As I totally submit myself to Thee!

Live in me! It's Your will I want to do!
Show me Jesus, how to bring others
To You!

Live in me Jesus! Show me how to walk
as You walked! Use my mouth, help me
to talk as You talked!

Live in me Jesus!

SEE ME!

I was born flesh of flesh and bone of bone,
As I now look around I stand all alone!

Walking the street with nowhere to go. Praying
that someone just a little love will show.

It's been so long since anyone looked into
my eyes. No one sees the many tears that
I cry!

I remember what it felt like to be touched. I
long for that feeling, how I miss it so much!

Lost in a crowd as though I'm the only one
there, searching for just one face that looks
like it may care!

Someone once spoke to me about a Savior
and how He died so I would be free! As I wander
the streets I look for that Savior in the many
eyes that don't see me!

STRETCHED

You stretched me Lord as You filled
my Spirit. You spoke to me and opened my
ears to hear it!

You stretched me beyond what I know.
You stretched me Lord, even when I
didn't want to go!

You showed me that You did not give me
the spirit of fear. But of strength and the
ability to stand and persevere.

You stretched me so that You I can please!
You stretch me not always standing,
sometimes You had to bring me to
my knees.

It is on my knees that I have grown the
most! Knowing that not on myself, but only
on You can I boast!

So, I thank You Lord for stretching me!
Beyond the limitations that my eyes can see!

THE FIRE WON'T GO OUT

There is a stirring in my soul, like fire shut up in
my bones! No matter how I try to ignore it, it
won't leave me alone!

What is this thing, this fire God put inside of me?
How do I bring it out so that others can see?

Is it a gift or is it a curse? The more I ignore it
it just gets worse!

There is a fire stirring way down in my soul and
I want to get it out! Sometimes it makes me want
to dance, sometimes I just want to shout!

Show me Lord how to embrace this fire and
use it for Your glory! Speak to me and let
me know how it fits into my life story.

Thank You for this fire Lord, I know it's coming
from You! Speak to me Lord, let me know what
I need to do!

There is a stirring in my soul, like fire shut up in my bones!

Jeremiah 20:8-10

THE LORD HAS NEED OF ME

The Lord has need of me! I fit into
His plan! He put something inside of
me, something He put in no other man.

The Lord has need of me, He wants me
to come now! I have to loose the ties that
bind me, have to shake them loose somehow!

I'm bound by doubt and guilt, by sin and
shame! Someone please uncover my mouth
I need to call on His name!

Loose the ropes that bind my hands, He has
work for me to do! I need to go where He leads
me, take the shackles from my feet too!

The Lord has need of me, but I need Him more!
Without Him I can do nothing, I stand bound
before an open door!

Where He has need of me, I don't know! I know
that if I trust Him, He will show me the way as I go!

The Lord has need of me, there is a stirring in my
soul! He wants me to come now, to stand and
be bold!

The Lord has need of me, I may have to go alone!
He put a dream inside of me, a dream that no
one else has been shown!

The Lord has need of me! I am stepping out on
faith! I want Him to say "Well done My child!"
when I reach that heavenly place!

The Lord Has Need of Me!!

TRUE LOVE

I have found my true love! A love like I
have never known. No greater love than
His can possibly be shown!

He makes me smile in spite of my tears. He
gives me peace and takes away my fears.

He holds me in His arms and tells me how much
He cares. He tells me that when I need Him He
will always be there.

He told me that He loved me before I knew who
He was. He was watching and waiting for me to see
Him and accept His love.

He whispers sweet words in my ear. Words I have
heard before but each time they are more clear.

He says that He will be all that I need Him to be!
If I will just trust Him He will take care of me.

I can't imagine my life without Him! He makes it
possible for me to breathe. With Him in my life I
can go through any trial with ease!

He turned my life around, put my feet on solid
ground!

And I fell in love!

WHO AM I?

Who am I but a child of God, created to do
His will! Who am I but a spirit with a
destiny to fulfill.

Who am I but a drop of sand, lost in a
great big sea. Lost until God decided
it was time for Him to use me!

He called my name, got my attention!
Somehow I knew it was time for me
to listen!

He told me to let go of things of the
flesh. Those temporary pleasures would
have my life in a mess!

He told me I could plan how my future
would be. But if I didn't check with Him
disappointment is all I would see.

Who am I but a breath from God, part of
His perfect plan. Formed from dirt to walk
this earth, formed by God's holy hands.

V
RELATIONSHIP

A LITTLE FURTHER

We must go a little further, beyond the raising of hands and
the saying of "Amen." Take us back to the old way let us
start again!

Back to stretching out beforeYou God! Allowing the Holy Spirit
to come in! Back to casting out demons and breaking yokes
by the laying on of hands.

Give us a deeper anointing, a higher level of praise. Let us
by Your power cure disease or even the dead let us raise!

Something more than structured religion where the preacher
is in control, let the Holy Spirit take over our praise like in
days of old!

Show us Lord how to go a little further beyond what we
now know! Take us behind the veil, and there more of
Your wisdom please show!

We must go further!

I Cor. 2:12-14

AWE

I'm in awe of You Father! And each day
that I live, shows me more and more
of the grace and mercy You so lovingly give!

You walk with me through struggles while
opening my eyes to see, that it's during
the struggles that You draw closer
and carry me!

You deliver me from situations when I
can see no way out. Helping me to understand
that what I learn on the walk through is what
it's all about!

You allow me to know You even though it's
only a glimpse of You I see! For You know that
I could not comprehend the full extent
of Your Majesty.

Father! I'm in awe of You! In awe of how You
love me, how You do the things that You do!
My sweet Heavenly Father! I am completely,
totally and lovingly in awe of You!

I Chronicles 29:11-12

COME AWAY WITH ME

God spoke to my heart and said "come away with Me!"
I have so much to tell you, there is so much I want you
to see!

Hold My hand, let's take a walk! Come away with Me
so we can talk!"

He talked to me about the mysteries of life! Told me
I should call on Him in times of strife!

He showed me mercy and gave me peace! Took
me to heights that on my own I could never reach!

He said "come away with Me, come spend some time.
I know about your concerns and I want to tell you Mine."

He is concerned about our lack of faith and how we have
put so many worldly things in His place!

He's concerned that we don't call on the Holy Spirit!
That when He gives us direction we don't know how
to hear it!

God is concerned about how we treat His creations!
The earth is moaning, there is decay in every nation.

He's concerned about how we treat one another.
Fathers against sons, daughters against their mothers!

God wants us to come away with Him, spend some
time in prayer. Don't be in a hurry, linger until He
meets you there!

Psalm 101:6

DEEPER

Take me deeper Lord. Deeper into Your Spirit.
Take me deeper, speak to me Lord. Your voice
I want to hear it.

I want to know what Your will is for my life. Take
Me deeper Lord, away from the confusion and strife.

Here is my heart Lord, I give it to You! I lay down
my will and I give You my life too!

Take me deeper!

Job 11:7-9

FOR ME

He died so that I might live.
Jesus died so that I might live.
My Savior died so that I might live.
His life He did freely give!

He allowed them to nail Him to the cross
and pierce Him in the side. For me He
gave His life, for me He bled and died!

The water and blood that flowed from His
side anoint me with His love. His nail
scarred hands are on my head giving me
guidance from above.

His feet that were scarred on the cross
now leave footprints in the sand as He
carries me when I'm not able to stand!

Now I in turn must die so that He can live
in me! I must step outside of myself
so it's only Him that you see!

I must walk as He walked, talk as He
talked, love and forgive as He did.
Study to show myself approved and
in my heart keep His word hid!

Jesus died so that I might live!
My Savior died so that I might live!
His life for me He did freely give!

1 Corinthians 15:1-4

GOD SMILES

To make God smile should be
your ultimate goal!
He smiles each time the magnitude
of His love for us is told.

He smiles when we His
love return. A passion for God
deep in your soul should burn!

God smiles when we give
Him our complete trust.
Rely on Him and Him alone,
it's not an option! We must!

God smiles when we are obedient
to His commands. Don't ask any questions,
in time you will understand.

God smiles when we continually
thank Him and give Him praise.
Don't be afraid to lift your voice
and holy hands to raise!

We were all given gifts and
different abilities! God smiles
when we use them so that others
can see!

There is nothing on this earth
that can bring you strife,
when making God smile is the
goal of your life!

Jesus Keeps Hanging Around

Jesus just keeps hanging around, no matter
how much I let Him down.

He hides me from all evil, He guides me when
I feel lost. He loves me when I'm unlovable.
Won't let me go at any cost.

He holds me back only when it's for my good.
He came to my rescue when no one else could.

Thank You Jesus for hanging around!

Romans 8:38-39

Married To The Holy Spirit

I'm married to the Holy Spirit!
It's for His pleasure that I live!

I've taken a vow to love Him.
My heart, soul and mind to give!

I'm married to the Holy Spirit!
I'm at His beck and call.
If I listen and do what He tells
me I know He won't let me fall!

He waited patiently for me, then
showed me what it's like to be loved!
A love blessed by my Heavenly Father,
a love that could only come from
heaven above!

He walks with me wherever I go. He
opens doors for me, He pushes aside
obstacles I may not be able to see!

I go to Him with questions, the answers
He freely gives! While helping me to
understand life, He advises me on
how I should live!

When my eyes stray to another and
unfaithful I become, He forgives me
when I confess and back into His
arms I am able to run!

I'm married to the Holy Spirit! He
gives me all I need. All He asks
in return is that I honor God and
His word I heed!

I'm married to the Holy Spirit! He will
never cheat on me, forsake me or
break my heart! I'm married to the
Holy Spirit, even in death we will never part!

MORE OF YOU

I want more of You Lord in my life in every way!
More glory and anointing, more love, peace
and grace!

Have Your way in me no matter where I may be!
In my home or on my job, please have Your way
in me!

Fill me up Lord, Fill me till I want no more! Fill me
to overflowing, so that others can see my joy!

I want more of You Lord!

RAGGEDY BIBLE MAN

God send me a "Raggedy Bible Man", a man who
studies Your word. A man who follows Your direction
and Your voice he has heard!

Send me a "Raggedy Bible Man" with whom I can
grow and give You praise! A man who is not afraid
his holy hands to raise.

Send me a man who is filled with Your spirit, and
can share Your Word with me. Then God give me
an ear to hear it!

A man who has shown himself approved and is totally
submitted to You! A "Raggedy Bible Man" that I
know will be true!

I want a man who loves You Lord more than he loves
me. A "Raggedy Bible Man" whose faith has set
him free!

I want a "Raggedy Bible Man" But! I want You more!
So draw me closer to You Lord until my "Raggedy
Bible Man" walks through the door!

Psalm 37:3-5

THE PRIVILEGE OF PRAYER

Prayer, what a privilege it is!
One of the greatest gifts that our
Father gives!

We can go to Him and take all
of our cares! We can dwell in His
presence anytime, anywhere!

We don't need an appointment or
to wait in line. He is never too busy
to answer your call or mine!

He loves when we call on Him, it
makes Him smile. He knew the call
was coming though it may have
taken awhile!

Just call and give Him some praise. He
already knows what we need! That
topic we don't even have to raise!

Direct access to the "Great I AM!" He
is that He is! and always will be!
What a privilege that He's always
available to you and me!

Prayer! Don't take it for granted or let
any opportunity pass. For we never know
if that opportunity will be our last.

Prayer What a Privilege!

TOSSING AND TURNING

Tossing and turning, no rest in sight!
Waking up tired like I've been in a fight
Wrestling like Jacob with something I can't see,
wondering who this is in bed with me.

Did I pray before I laid down, and confess all my sins?
Is this thing that I'm wrestling with coming from within?

Then I remember, we fight not against flesh and blood
but against demons and spirits from high places.

The Bible says that if we resist the devil he will flee!
So I'm going to use the authority God gave to me!

I'll keep on my armor day and night, so I'm always ready
if these spirits want to fight!

I must examine my life, see how this thing
with no face got in. What door did I leave open,
why did this thing think it could be my friend?

I want to wake up in the morning and be able to say,
I had a peaceful sleep last night, slept without a worry or a care.
I had a peaceful sleep last night
because the presence of the Lord was there.

Who is sleeping in your bed!
Do you have peace when you lay down?

VI
ENCOURAGEMENT

NEVER GIVE UP

Never give up, no matter how hard the fight.
Never give up call on Jesus depend on His might.

Never give up stand your ground, when things
seem hopeless God can turn them around!

There is help waiting if you humble yourself! God
has a way out. Never give up and put your dream
on a shelf.

Don't lose hope! Jesus is the hope for our souls!
Never give up!

Psalm 130:4-6

PEACE BE STILL

When the storms of life are raging and you don't know
what to do, look up and see the glory of God, let His
Spirit minister to you!

He is God almighty, the great I AM, Master of all the
land. He spoke everything into existence and can end
it with the wave of His hand!

He raised the dead, and made the lame to walk, gave
the blind eyes to see! With just a thought He can fix
whatever your problem might be!

He said to the wind, "peace be still" and it had no choice
but to obey, as He calmed an angry sea! If He can do
all of that there is no limit to what He can do for you and me!

One touch of His hand can change your life story!
"Peace be still!" Look up and see His glory!

"Peace be still" all power is in His hands!
He came to make
all things new, "peace be still" as He now does that
for you!

He knew your situation before it came to be. Whatever
your concerns are, just remember your God parted a sea!

"Peace be still" and see the glory of God! "Peace be still"

Philippians 4:6-9

SUDDENLY

The last bit of grain and only a
few drops of oil. Seems there is never
enough no matter how hard you toil!

Then suddenly out of nowhere comes
everything you need! Not just enough for
you, but others you are also able to feed!

Sometimes you're backed in a corner and you
don't know what to do, then suddenly there's
a door and a guide to show you through!

When your body is consumed with pain
and the doctors, they give up! Then suddenly
you begin to feel something like a sweet
heavenly touch!

When the doctors are puzzled and say
they don't understand! Tell them,
"it's a God thing", tell them that you
know a Man!

A Man named Jesus! The Son of the
Great I AM!

A Doctor that a degree can't name!
Tell them that He came to earth and
took on all of your pain!

Whatever the need is in your life, that
is what He will be! Call on Him and
watch for your "Suddenly!"

VII
DIRECTION

DISCERNING SPIRIT

Lord give me a discerning spirit to know when
You are talking to me. Give me a discerning
spirit to understand the things that I see.

A spirit of expectancy, obedience and faith.
A spirit that is worthy of one day beholding
Your face.

As the Holy Spirit guides me, let wisdom be
my friend. A friend that walks with me until
my journey ends!

Lord give me a discerning spirit!

I Corinthians 12:7-11

HEAR OUR CRY

So many spirits crying out,
lost and in despair!
So many looking for answers and
no one seems to care!

The world is in such turmoil!
We've lost sight of You!
Help us Lord! We need Your
help if we are to make it through!

We have lived our lives so carelessly!
Our morals thrown aside!
Hide us from ourselves Lord!
It's in You we must abide!

Take us to Your shelter!
There we will find rest!
Cover us with Your shadow,
walk with us through each test!

Our spirits cry for we lack
true knowledge of You!
Take us to the beginning Lord,
Let us start anew!

Forgive us for our iniquities,
purge us of our sins.
Send the Holy Spirit, show
us how to let Him in!

So many spirits crying out,
lost and in despair!
Help us remember You are
the answer and Your love is
always there!

It's Not About Me

I sit, I wait, I pray
and contemplate.
If only I knew God's plan
if only I knew my fate!

Decisions I have made,
paths I have taken.
Could I have made the wrong
turn, been totally mistaken?

Did I ask God what He wanted,
what His choice for me was?
Did I stop to talk to Him, to make
sure that the directions were coming
from above?

As I grow closer to God, as through
these eyes I more clearly see,
I realize that this thing called
"my life" has nothing to
do with me!

It's about You, Jesus, it's about
Your unconditional love.
It's about grace, mercy and
all gifts that come from above!

It's about me living my life in a
way that honors You!
It's about giving You praise for
all that You allow me to do!

It's about lifting You up so that
others can see,
The Holy Spirit that protects
and abides in me!

It's about learning how to
hear Your voice!
Knowing that if I will just listen
You will lead me to the right choice!

It's about faith the size of
a mustard seed.
It's about knowing that
with it, You will take care
of my every need!

It's about stepping forward when
You have given me a task,
and knowing You will supply,
no need for me to ask!

It's about me being able to
stand and testify!
That it was for sinners like me
You were willing to die!

It's about knowing and nurturing
the gift given me.
About sharing that gift with
others and praising Thee!

I now know that I should continue
to sit, wait, pray and contemplate.
But not worry about Your plan for me,
not be concerned with my fate!

So humble me Lord! I strive
to be still!
Humble me, and help me to walk
in Your perfect will!

Because I now know, IT'S NOT ABOUT ME!!

Galatians 2:20

NEW BEGINNING

A new beginning! A changing of the guard. The
passing on of wisdom through the connection of hearts!

A new beginning, stepping out on faith a destiny to fulfill!
Anointed for God's purpose, anointed to do His will.

A new beginning, a season of change. A time to move
forward and see what new thing life will bring!

As the old law passed away and Christ took its place,
life brings new beginnings each day full of God's
mercy and grace.

For everything there is a season, nothing stays the
same! As the sun rises and the moon fades away,
God gives us new beginnings each and every day!

Step into your new beginning knowing that God will help
you stand. If you but keep your eyes on Him,
He will work His plan through your hand!

EMBRACE YOUR NEW BEGINNING!

Colossians 3:9-10

OPEN MY EYES

Open my eyes Lord, so that I may see,
all the wonderful things You
want to reveal to me.

Help me not be distracted, or
take my focus from You.
Give me understanding of what
You want me to do.

Strengthen my mind Lord so
that I might retain Your word.
Then share it with others
who have not heard.

Not heard of Your goodness,
Your mercy and grace.
Not heard that with You any
obstacle they can face!

Open my eyes Lord, so that I may see,
all the wonderful things You
want to reveal to me!

SPIRIT OF TRUTH

"The Lord is nigh unto all them that call upon Him, to all that call upon Him in Truth."

Psalms 145:18

Lord give us the Spirit of Truth as we draw closer to You!
Fill us with Your Spirit Lord,
show us what You would have us do.

We seek that truth that sets us free to worship according to
Your will. Your presence in all we do is
what we want to feel.

Spirit of Truth bring wisdom, peace, discernment and love!
Help us to move according to Your will,
guide us from above.

We know Lord that You are the Way, the Truth and the Life. Cover us
with Your blood, protect us from all strife.

Spirit of Truth make us holy. Teach us Your word, so that we can
minister to those who have not heard.

Spirit of Truth come sit with us each and every day! We know that if
we honor You, nothing can stand in our way!

We seek You, Spirit of Truth! make Your presence known, a church
without spot or wrinkle is what we strive to be.
Fill us with Your Spirit so that You in us is what the world
will see!

Lord give us the Spirit of Truth!

John 4:23-24

FEAR, FLESH AND FOLK

Fear is a spirit that God did not give us, He said it in His word!
"Fear not for I am with thee, fear not stand still and see." If we but
trust in what God says how much easier our lives would be!

Fear comes from the enemy, those principalities that we must fight
every day. They want to keep us bound and operating in our flesh so
they can have their way!

We must bind our flesh daily, and listen for God's voice, discern the
difference between folk and our Father, know which will lead us to
the right choice!

Folk will try and convince you that they know what's best for you,
when most folk have things in their own lives for which they don't
know what to do!

Fear, flesh and folk! On their own they are bad enough, put them
together and they can really make your life rough!

Fear, flesh and folk! What a deadly combination!

TO BE CALLED BY MY NAME

Oh! to be called by my name,
to clearly Lord hear Your voice!
To feel Your presence all around me,
to know that my actions are
Your choice.

Like Saul on the road to Damascus
was changed, it is my desire Lord
that only Your will remains!

Sift me of all ungodly things, show
me the way to go. Sift me Lord so
that the Holy Spirit in me is all
that's left to show!

Give me understanding Lord, help
me to think as You do. Every step
that I take let it be ordered by You!

Isaiah 45:3-5

WHISPERS

God help me to hear the whispers as You speak
to me! That small still voice that will set me free.

Free from the things that bind me and keep me
from victory. Free to be all that You want me to be!

Help me to hear the whispers telling me which
way to go. The loving whispers of Your Spirit full
of wisdom and all that I need to know!

God help me to hear the whispers! I want to live
with my ear against Your lips!

Proverbs 2:1-5

VIII
Dependence

Carry Me Lord!

Are You trying to get my attention Lord?
If so, that You have done.
I am listening, knowing that whatever it is
this race You will help me run!

My children are so dear to me! My life
for them I would give!
Help me understand Your will, and
each day for You to live.

Adversities, I've had a few, have dealt
with losses I didn't understand!
Through it all I tried not to lose sight
of You, not to let go of Your
unchanging hand!

When weakness overcomes me
because my spirit is so weary!
Remind me to call on Your name, I know
You are standing by me to carry!

When my heart becomes so burdened
that I think I can't go on,
help me to remember, one word from
You will make me strong!

You are carrying me right now Lord,
for I surely don't know what to do!
You are carrying me right now Lord,
I'm depending totally on You!

So help me to stand Lord,
and not waiver in my faith!
Until You say, "Well done My child,
You have reached your resting place!"

Matthew 11:28-29

CLOSER WALK WITH THEE

I hunger for a closer walk,
a closer walk with Thee!
I hunger Lord to hear Your voice
as You give direction to me!

I only want to do Your will,
walk in Your grace each day!
Guide my footsteps Father,
show me Your holy way!

I stumble when I step out on my own,
I can't make this journey without You!
Fill me with Your Spirit Lord! Show
me what You would have me do!

It's not about the things I want,
my earthly desires are few!
It's about making You smile Father,
and living my life to please You!

Sometimes my soul silently cries out
because I have lost sight of You!
I humble myself seeking Your face, until
Your presence shines through.

Feed me with Your mercy Lord!
Anoint me with Your love!
Let every step that I take
be ordered from above!

I hunger for a closer walk.
A closer walk with Thee!

Psalm 86:10-12

I'm Holding On

You are taking me somewhere Lord,
where I don't understand!
I know that to make it I must hold on
to Your unchanging hand!

I pray that soon my destination
You will show.
Until that time I'm holding on Lord!
I'm afraid to let go!

Things seem out of order now,
not the way they should be!
Each time I take a step I know it's
only because You are carrying me!

So, carry me Lord and on the way
let me see,
that in all I go thru there is a
lesson just for me!

A divine lesson of courage, faith,
dedication and love!
A lesson sent straight from
Heaven above!

So, I'll continue on this path Lord,
when I get tired, Please carry me!
For where my destination is I can
only get there by submitting
myself to Thee!

Carry Me Lord!

Proverbs 3:5-6

87

IX
CONFIDENCE

APPLE OF HIS EYE

I am the apple of His eye, and I know that!
For me He bled and died, and I know that!

He set a path for me to follow and walks with
me along the way. He is my shelter, it's Him
that keeps me safe day to day!

He provides all my needs and doesn't ask much
in return. All the blessings are gifts from Him.
I have nothing that I have earned.

I am the apple of His eye!
And I know that!

Psalm 17:7-9

I Am Not An Accident

I am not an accident,
God wants me to be here!
He planned my entrance to
His world, knew exactly
what time I would appear!

He knew the color of my eyes,
how big they would be!
He knew everything there was
to know about this spirit
I call Me!

He set a path for me to follow,
knew that I would stray!
He had other spirits waiting
to help me find my way!

He allowed me to be a vessel
other spirits to guide in!
Gave me the charge of letting
them know that He is their
best friend!

I am not an accident,
I need to be here!
When God is ready, He
will make the reason clear!

I Know Too Much

You can't make me doubt Him, I know too much!
You can't make me turn from Him, I have experienced
His touch!

I have witnessed the miracle of His healing hands.
He did for someone I love what couldn't be done by man!

I know that He delivered me when there seemed to
be no way out! I know that it was His grace, in me
there is no doubt!

You can't make me doubt Him!
I know too much!

Numbers 23:19

I TRUST YOU LORD

I trust You Lord through sunshine
and through rain. I trust You Lord
when I'm happy or consumed
with pain!

I trust You Lord to walk with
me every day. To direct my
path and show me the way.

I trust You Lord even when
I cannot see! If I put my hand
in Yours I know You will
guide me!

Proverbs 3:5-6

LIGHT INSIDE OF ME

I can step into darkness with the light inside of me.
The light of the Holy Spirit makes it possible for me
to see!

I can step into dark places and the atmosphere will
change. I enter with hands raised and calling on
Jesus' name!

As I enter into darkness with the light inside of me,
souls are transformed, spirits are set free!

The lame begin to walk, the deaf begin to talk, blind
eyes are able to see! Thank You Holy Spirit for being
that light inside of me!

John 1:45

PSALM 27 "DWELL"

When the enemy attacks me, why should I run away?
The Lord is my light and salvation, He protects
me every day!

I shall not be afraid, because God did not give me a
spirit of fear. I stand fast in His presence as He
draws near.

I will dwell in that secret place, abide in His shadow,
take refuge under His wings! There I will be delivered
from whatever the enemy brings.

I will sing of His goodness, His name I will give praise!
I give myself as a living sacrifice for the rest of my days!

I want to dwell with Him forever in that heavenly place,
So when my earthly journey is over, I will meet Him face to face!

"One thing have I desired of the Lord, that will I seek after;
that I may dwell in the house of the Lord all the days of
my life, to behold the beauty of the Lord, and to inquire
in His temple."

Psalms 27: 4

SURRENDER SATAN

We've got you surrounded Satan! Going to
interrupt your flow! Your fate has been sealed
and you have nowhere to go!

We have surrounded you with prayer, blocked
your path with praise. If you turn to the left
or right you will find our holy hands raised!

We've got you surrounded satan! And there is
nothing you can do! We have had enough, your
time is up! We accept nothing else from you!

We've got you surrounded Satan! Surrender now!

Luke 10:19

TREE THAT I AM

Many storms have come, and mighty winds
have blown! But the tree that I am, I'm still
standing strong.

A tree, sprung from branches much stronger
than I. Taught how through the winds and
the storms to stand tall and survive.

Just one leaf hanging from the tree of my
life. Nurtured by the dew that fell from my
ancestors eyes.

A tree now full gown with branches springing
from me. Teaching them to stand and through
the storms to have victory.

Through the storms I sway, may even have to
bend! But with each sway I find strength
coming from within!

After each storm is over, again I stand tall!
No matter how strong the winds my God
won't let me fall!

As the winds come and go, my faith will
not waiver! My branches reaching high like
holy hands, I give praise to my Savior!

The Tree That I Am Standing Tall!

Isaiah 40:31

WEAPON OF MASS DESTRUCTION

A weapon of mass destruction, a power beyond
compare! There is nothing that can stand against
you when you use the privilege of prayer!

When fiery darts come at you, when evil spirits
attack, fall on your knees and call on Jesus He
always has your back!

When Satan tries to set you up, tries to interrupt
your flow! Pull out your weapon of mass
destruction and tell the devil "No!"

Principalities coming from high places, know
that it's not your fight. Just pray in the name
of Jesus, no evil can stand under His might!

When sickness attacks your body, remember
Jesus shed His blood for that! Just call Him
accept and expect your healing. He took it
all on His back!

When situations seem hopeless and you don't
know what to do, don't worry, just give praise
to your Savior and He will take care of it for you!

Prayer is a weapon of mass destruction! Use it!

YOU CAN'T TELL ME

Don't try and tell me my God isn't real!
Don't try and tell me that it's not
His presence that I feel!

That soft touch that wakes me after
watching over me all night.
That comforting voice that tells me
everything will be alright.

Don't try and tell me that God won't
be there. To take away every worry,
take away every care!

You can't tell me that God won't give
me the victory! Don't try and tell me
that His blood didn't set me free!

Don't try and tell me that my God isn't
real! In times of trouble I know it's His
presence I feel!

X
CONTEMPLATION

Ancestors Speak

Listen! I hear the voice of our ancestors!
They want to remind us what they went through!
Because of them we now have the freedom to do all
that we are able to do!

They want to remind us that freedom
has never been free!
They say!

We came through many dangers, many toils
and snares. But we made it through because
God was always there!

We sung the songs that gave us hope. We couldn't
read but we learned to pray. We prayed Heavenly
Father, help us make it through one more day!

We took the stripes on our back, we cried and
we bled. Each stripe took us closer to our Lord.
Each stripe removed the crowns from our heads!

We could only watch as our families were torn
apart. Sold as pieces of meat, each sale took a
piece of our hearts!

Beaten, hung, burned and raped, forced to give
birth! They called us animals, trying to strip
us of our self-worth!

But we rose above all they would do, our
dignity still intact! By the grace of God
we made it through, learned how to
survive in lack!

Somehow our great-grandchildren's children's,
children have completely lost their way!

No one
told them about the Kings and Queens we were
before we were bound and drug away!

Away from our land of milk and honey, of riches
still untold!
Away from everything we knew to
be stripped naked, put on a block and sold!

Someone please tell the children at what price
they are free to do what they do! Let them know that
when they kill one another it pierces our hearts
through and through!

Let them know that every time they use the N word
another stripe is added to our backs! Tell them that
we walked so far so they would not have to live like that!

Every time a father walks away from his child that
selling block is rebuilt! and the scream of a mother
can be heard for miles!

Every time our women sell their bodies for drugs
or cash, the slaves that would not submit to the master
take on one more lash!

Someone please talk to the children! Don't let our
suffering be in vain! Tell them by the grace of God
we made it through. Let them know that they can
do the same!

SOMEONE PLEASE TALK TO THE CHILDREN!
PLEASE! SOMEONE TALK TO THE CHILDREN!
PLEASE! TALK TO THE CHILDREN!

AUDACITY

We have been making history since time began. Through
all of our suffering God always had us in His plan!

Because of the audacity of hope we now rise to take
our place. Once again God has shown us His grace.

Grace that brought us through slavery to a land called
"free." Rising from bondage we now stand in victory.

The audacity of hope from a man born for a time such
as this. Easing the heartache of a people for so long
suppressed.

The audacity to dream and believe that dreams can
come true. Black man stand and take your place, hope for so
many has come through you!

God said the first will be last and the last will
be first. I now see clearly what was meant
by that verse!

From slavery to the White House, from bondage to
victory! The audacity of hope for the world to see!

EVEN TIDE

The women are travailing, crying out in despair.
We look around we can't see our men,
can't find them anywhere!

We need You Lord to hear our cries, our
troubled souls to keep! We need You Lord
to help us, this despair goes so deep!

Our families are in turmoil, our children
are in pain! They are killing one another!
Our nurturing seems to have been in vain!

Is it even tide? Where are our men? Are they
off to war or just asleep? Are they looking
for us to nurture them? Their souls do they
expect us to keep?

We are on our knees, we lay prostrate on our
face! Crying out to You Lord, so grateful
for Your amazing grace!

Your grace that is sufficient, Your grace
that is so sweet! We need for our men
to lead us as we bow humbly at Your feet!

Is it even tide? Our men are not here!
Their children are looking for them too!
They wonder, "does my daddy even care?"

Speak to the hearts of our men Lord! There
is no time to spare! The sun will soon be rising
and we need for our men to be there!

Is it even tide? Where are our men?

2 Samuel 11

GOD SCREAMS AT AMERICA

God is screaming at America, the
land of the free! He's screaming for us
to open our eyes and see what our end
will be!

We've turned our backs on Him, we've
prostituted ourselves! The motto "In God
we trust" has been boxed up and put on
a shelf!

We've placed ourselves in bondage!
Idol gods everywhere. The things that
are most important are the things we give
the least care!

Our children are being sacrificed to appease
our lustful flesh! We've created a modern day
Babylon, America we are not giving God our best!

The sky is so polluted we can now see the air
we breathe! God is screaming at us America! In
us He is not well pleased!

Houses, cars, fortune and fame, we worship
these while God in a box on a shelf remains!

God's wrath is upon us America! What is
it going to take? Tsunami's, tornadoes, fires!
God screams and the earth quakes!

We use God's name so casually, taking it
in vain! If we don't turn back to Him how
much longer can we remain?

Terrorists are coming at us, God has opened
the door, He's allowing America to feel the
pain He protected us from before!

God is screaming at us America! Screaming
louder every day! He wants us to turn back to
Him, walk in the narrow way!

People living under bridges, while others play
on yachts! The gap is getting wider between
the haves and the have not's!

God is screaming at America, we must remove
Him from the box we put Him in! Fall prostrate
at His feet, ask Him to forgive us of our sins!

God is screaming at us America! We must open
our ears to hear! He's screaming for our attention
warning us that the end draws near!

God is screaming at America!
The land of the free?
Without God how much
freedom can there really be?

God is screaming at us America!
Screaming louder every day!

Ezekiel 20:7-9

KATRINA

You are showing us Yourself Lord, You
have opened our eyes to see what a
blessing the storms in our lives can be!

The wind and rain washed so much away!
An entire city destroyed in one day!

Families separated, small children on their
own! I wonder, do they know that You never
left them alone?

So many stories of pain, anguish, fear and
despair! Do they know Lord that through it
all, You were always there?

You said if we would humble ourselves, confess
our sins, seek Your face and pray! That You
would heal our land and forgive our sins.
Is that what You are doing today?

So many blessings on the other side of
this storm! So many testimonies of how You
held them in Your arms!

You have bought us all together Lord, we've
opened up our hearts! We're loving one
another, so many trying to do their part!

Let us not forget and go back to our old ways!
Help us to always love one another and honor
You for the rest of our days!

LITERACY

The Word of God is precious!
When you hear it, it sounds so sweet.
To understand its meaning is a gift we
can all receive.

Literacy enables us to read God's word,
study to get understanding and confirm the
things we have heard.

Literacy will open doors that may have been
closed before. Give us special revelations
from God as He reveals Himself to us more
and more!

Literacy, it's a right! Make it your choice!

LOOK ON US!

Do our children stand a chance with
us in control? A chance not just to
prosper, but a chance to grow old!

We have destroyed the very foundation
of what God provided for us! Lost
sight of the motto "In God We Trust"

Can't breathe the air, drink the water
or eat the food! We don't need education!
Let's close up some of these schools!

Look on us Father! Forgive us of our
sins! Remove the evil we have let in!

Men marrying men, women doing the
same. It's ok to do that just don't call
on Jesus' name!

They want us to cover our heart and
salute the flag, but not to mention the
name of God! Since He is the Creator
who gave us a heart, something about
that to me seems so odd!

Look on us Father! We know not what we do!
Bring us back into fellowship with you!

What about the generations to come,
they deserve the same chance as us!
We need to pray that they will do better
and get back to "In God We Trust."

Look On Us Father!

MARY HOW DID YOU DO IT?

Mary how did you do it? How did you stay so
strong? While they persecuted your Son when you
knew He had done no wrong.

How did you follow Him as He carried that cross?
Did you know He carried it for you and for all who
would be lost?

Did you see the sin He carried as they nailed His feet
and hands? Did you know your presence there gave
Him the strength to stand.

Mary did you know what He meant when He said,
"I make all things new!" When He asked His Father
to forgive them, Mary I wonder if you knew.

When they hung Him high and stretched Him wide,
Mary did you know, that salvation could be had by
all through the Blood that from His body flowed.

Mary, how did you do it, how did you stay so strong?
When He was born flesh of your flesh and bone of
your bone.

When He defeated death and walked away from the
grave, did you know of the souls that would be saved?

Mary, I want to thank you for being willing to carry
my Savior! Because of your obedience I can now walk
in God's favor!

John 19:25-30

OUR CHILDREN

Our babies are having babies and throwing
them away! Our daughters are searching for love,
and accepting love expressed in the wrong way!

Our sons are selling drugs, using scooters on which
they use to play. They are hanging out on street
corners, carrying guns and blowing each other away!

Our children are using the colors of the flag; the
red and the blue. They are terrorizing communities
because they have nothing else to do !

We're taking money from the schools, building
bigger and better jails! It's as though we're
telling our children, "You can all go to hell!"

Mothers get off the street corners, leave the
men and drugs alone! Get yourselves together,
show your children what it is like to have a home!

Fathers, wake up and pay attention! Our children
also need your love! God gave you charge over
your family, if you don't know how seek guidance
from above!

What are we doing to each other? Men and women
can't communicate! We're looking to people of the
same sex, calling them our mates!

We can't control our own flesh! No wonder our
children are in such a mess!

We have to save our children, show them a better
way! Talk to them about our Savior, about His love,
mercy and grace.

God said that if we would call on Him, humble
ourselves, turn from our wicked ways, seek His
face and pray, that He would heal our land and
forgive our sins. We need to stop and call on Him today!

2 Chronicles 7:14

113

STEP OUTSIDE

If I step outside of myself then turn
and look back in, would I see someone
there that I would want to call my friend.

Do I see someone that's loving, someone
gentle and kind. Would I be happy to
have the heart that I see? Proud to
say that it's mine!

Or would I see hatred, jealousy, envy
and lust. Is the heart that I see one
that I would trust.

When I step outside of myself, would
I want to step back in. If I take a good
look will I be able to see all of the
un-confessed sin.

How blessed we are to serve a God
who looks beyond your flesh! He sees
what's deep inside our hearts, and loves
us despite our sin that's un-confessed!

THE CROSS

Have you really thought about the Cross?
About what our salvation really cost.

God lowered Himself to humanity, so
that all of our trials He could see as
we see!

He was condemned for sin in which He
had no part. In return all He asked is
that we let Him into our hearts!

His love for us is stronger than the
death He walked through! His love
is so amazing and given freely
to sinners like me and you!

Have you thought about His stripes
that heal? Those stripes are His love
for us revealed!

Have you really thought about the Cross
and what it did for you?

WAKE UP

It's time to wake up now! We've been asleep
too long! Time to wake up and see what
in the world is going on.

The clock is ticking, time is drawing nigh.
Time to wake up, there's a rumbling in the sky!

We have to wake up! And wipe the sleep from
our eyes. We need to see clearly if we
are to survive!

We need to fast, pray and consecrate ourselves!
We must change our sinful ways and take
God off the shelf!

We must wake up! God is doing a new thing!
Wake up! And open your eyes least ye be deceived
and fall for Satan's schemes!

Why don't you wake up! God is trying to shake us
from our sleep! It's almost time for us our
Redeemer to meet!

His hand is on the door, it will open soon!
When it does you don't want to be asleep!
Asleep in some dark room!

We have taken so much for granted! We have
forgotten who sent us here! We all have a mission
to fulfill, the final hour is drawing near!

It's time to wake up!

Romans 13:10-12
Ephesians 5:13-15

WELL DONE MY CHILD

What drives your life?
What do you hold dear?

Does it help you accomplish the
purpose for which God put you here?

Are you driven by guilt, holding
on to the past?
Turn it over to Jesus and have
perfect peace at last!

Resentment, anger and
also fear,
keep you separated from God.
He wants you to come near!

Are you driven by material
things? These things will pass away!
Make God the focus of your life,
what He offers will forever stay!

Are you concerned with what
others think of you; Trying to
please everyone?
There is no lasting reward for either
of these, when your life on earth is done.

Be driven by the will of God!
His purpose to fulfill!
He is the one you should
strive to please, the only One to
whom you should kneel!

Be driven by the will of God!
Hold His commandments dear!
"Well done my good and faithful child!"
In the end is what you will hear!

Matthew 25:21

WHY?

I asked God "why?" Why do I suffer and have so
much pain? Why does every good thing in my life
seem to always change!

Why do I feel so lonely and no one seems to care?
When others were in need, wasn't I always there?

Why is my life so empty when not long ago it was
so full? If you hear me God, please tell me why!
Have I broken some holy rule?

God answered me and said, "Yes, I hear you calling
My name! You want to know why you suffer, why
you are in so much pain!

While I have your attention, I have some questions
too! Do you even know who I am? Or realize all
the things I have done for you?

Did you ask me "why" when I woke you this morning
and gave you a brand new day? Did you ask "why"
when I walked with you through problems when
you couldn't see your way?

Did you ask "why" I blessed you with resources
beyond your need! And all I ask in return is that
you love Me and My word you heed?

When was the last time you read My word? The
answers to your questions are there! When
you didn't have these problems did you stop
and say "Thank You" and tell Me how much
you care?

Tell me, why are there people starving, when
you have food to eat? Why are you able to
have shoes to wear, when someone has no feet?

Don't you know I created you? It's My breath
that you breathe? Have you done anything to
honor Me? Do you deserve the blessings you
have received?

You look for people and things to fill your life,
you've left no room for Me! Open your heart
and let Me in and your "why's" will be turned
to Praise and Victory!"

Psalm 55:1-2

WOMB TO TOMB

What happens between the womb and the
tomb that keeps our lives in sin? Why
does it take us so long to find that
Holy Spirit within?

What happens that keeps us from
remembering what we once knew, before
our spirit was poured into flesh and in
our mother's womb we grew?

Why do we let "lust of the flesh, lust of
the eyes and the pride of life" linger
in our lives and cause us so much strife?

What happens between the womb and the
tomb that keeps us from hearing God's voice?
The voice that will always guide us and help
us make the right choice?

Do we return to the womb when we enter the
tomb and our knowledge become refreshed?
Realizing that the divine nature of God has
walked with us through the whole process!

"Life" happens between the
womb and the tomb!

XI
COMMITMENT

BEFORE THE THRONE

When you stand before the throne of God what will
your answers be? When He asks "what did you do
with My Son? can you say that you told someone
how He could set them free?

When it is your turn to give an account for the life
that you have lived, will you be able to stand proudly
before the King and say
"the best that I had I did give."

We all will be accountable for the things that we have done.
Will you be able to say that you shared
Jesus and God's amazing grace with someone?

Must Jesus bear the cross alone and all of us go free?
Or will you share the cross with Him no
matter how heavy it may be?

We will be accountable for every word that we say,
every deed that we do! So as we walk through this
thing called life, please pray for me and I will pray
for you!

When you stand before the throne of God, what will
your answers be?

DISCIPLESHIP

Holy Spirit endow us so that we can do God's
will. Create in us clean hearts so our purpose we
can fulfill.

We can't do it without You Holy Spirit, we need
You to prepare the way. Then give us holy boldness
and the right words to say.

The world is in such turmoil, death and destruction
everywhere. So many deceived by the devil's
schemes. Help us to give them God's word and
let them know You are there.

Prepare the hearts of those to whom we are sent.
We know they can't hear unless You call. Gird
up our legs as we go so that we can stand and
please catch us if we begin to fall.

Help us stand firm wearing the Belt of Truth and
the Breastplate of Righteousness, our feet fitted
with the Gospel of Peace. We will carry the Shield
of Faith so that we are protected from the flaming
arrows reach.

The Helmet of Salvation upon our heads, the Sword
of the Spirit in or hands. If You go with us Holy
Spirit we know we will be able to stand.

No matter how hard it may be or how long it may
take, we cannot tire of our efforts or lose our faith.

We must finish the course set before us, there is no
other way. So we put on the full armor of God and
with Your help Holy Spirit we will stand and spread
the Good News every day!

How You Living?

The day will come when you will breathe no more!
When the spirit of death will come knocking at your
life's door!

When your spirit will wake up in a different place.
Will it be a place of torment or a place of grace?

So I ask you now, how are you living? Your very
best to God are you giving?

How are you living?

Ezekiel 18:30-32

PURPOSE

There is a purpose for everything
in life. Each trial that we go through,
is designed to get us to that place
where we can be made new.

To worship God is why we are here,
to glorify His name!
worship Him without ceasing and
your life will be forever changed!

To be a member of God's own
family, to fellowship with others
who believe, is one of the greatest
privileges that we can ever receive!

We must become disciples, be
more like Christ each day!
Reflecting His glory, striving to
be like Him in every way!

God shaped us from the inside
out, His purpose to fulfill.
To minister to each other,
hold someone's hand as
they climb that hill!

He gave us the work of
spreading the good news!
Evangelists we must be.
Open the eyes of others who
may not be able to see!

God made us just to love us,
this life is preparation
for eternity!
Commit your life to the purposes
of God, and after each trial
more like Him you will be!

Romans 8:28-29

SPIRIT WITHIN

Spirit inside this temple I call Me!
When I look into my eyes it's You
I want to see!

Show me Spirit what others see, when
they look through the windows of this
temple I call me!

Are the windows clean so that
others can see through?
Have I done all I can to take
care of You?

Have I fed You with the fruits of
the Spirit? Shown love, kindness
and faithfulness, shared Your word
so that others can hear it?

Spirit that dwells inside of me,
show me what You want
others to see when they look
into the windows of this temple
I call me!

STAND AND FIGHT

The world is in such turmoil, trouble everywhere!
People hungry and homeless, so much pain and
despair!

Lies and deception are the order of the day! The
very ground we walk on is now in decay!

No matter how hard it may be or how long it may
take, I cannot grow weary in my efforts or lose my faith!

I must finish the course set before me, there is no
other way! So I put on the full armor of God and
fight on every day!

I stand firm wearing the belt of truth, and the breastplate of
righteousness, my feet fitted with the gospel of peace!
I carry the shield of faith so that I am protected from the
flaming arrows reach!

The helmet of salvation upon my head, the sword of
the Spirit in my hands. If I pray without ceasing I know
I will be able to stand!

John 16:33

XII
REPENTANCE

BACK TO YOU

My life has been full of struggles, I now
turn it back over to You! Trusting You
Lord to lead me, change my heart, make
it like new!

I'm turning my life back over to You, Your
purpose to fulfill. Help me Lord to walk it
out to do what is Your will!

I give my life back to You!

Luke 9:23-24

COME ON IN

When life has overwhelmed you and you
don't know what to do, just come on in
to Jesus, He's waiting to counsel you!

When life seems out of order, hang on, a
change is going to come. Just take your
attention from your problem and focus
on the Holy One!

Give Him all your troubles, He knows
just what to do! If you will let go and
let Him, He will do what's best for you!

Come on in, the door is always open!

Matthew 11:27-29

COME TO MYSELF

I have come to myself! God has
let me see that there is so much
more that He has for me!

If I humble myself and just come
home! God is waiting to welcome
me no matter how long I've been gone!

He will run out to meet me! And give
me the best of what He has! If I just
confess, my sins will be part of my past!

I have come to myself and I'm home to
stay! Never again will I choose to go astray!

Luke 15: 17-20

FIX ME

Fix me Holy Spirit, clean me up! Heal me Holy Spirit
by Your loving touch!

Fix me Holy Spirit! Fix my sin stained heart. Make
it pure again where sin has turned it dark!

Renew in me a clean spirit, make me like new!
Fix me Holy Spirit I want to be more like You!

Fix Me Holy Spirit!

Psalm 51:9-11

EYES OF MY PARENTS

Life is a beautiful cycle, and with age I begin to see,
that when I look in the mirror it's the eyes of my parents
looking back at me.

All of the things that my parents would say, little did I know
I would be echoing them one day!

As a mother and a grandmother I can now clearly see that
when my parents said "no!" it was all about loving me.

Through the eyes of my parents I'm now able to lead the
way to salvation and living in God's will each day.

As I look at my children, and their children look at me,
I know that one day when they look in the mirror, it's
my eyes they will see.

Psalm 34:17-18

XIII
COMFORT

BE HAPPY FOR ME

Be happy for me, my journey is done!
My spirit is set free and real joy has begun.

Cry if you must, I know you will miss my presence,
but be happy for me I'm now walking around heaven!

I have seen the rainbow that encircles God's throne,
talked with the 24 elders, they welcomed me home!

Be happy for me! No more sorrow or pain do I feel.
I have seen the real glory of God and I know that He
is real!

Thank you for walking through my life with me. The
love we shared was so deep! So, be happy for me,
I now bow down at the Master's feet!

I have joined the angels singing "Holy, Holy, Holy is
The Lord God Almighty who was and is and is to come."
Be happy for me my journey is done!

I finished my course so God called me home and I had to
leave you there. I pray that I left you sweet memories of
the good times we shared!

I loved you with all that I could and I know that you
loved me too! So be happy for me my time on earth
is through!

All my questions have been answered,
life's mysteries have been made so clear! The
greatest gift you can give
me now is to meet me here!

Be Happy For Me!

2 Timothy 4:6-8

DRY BONES

It is by God that all things consist!
He holds all things together; without
Him nothing can exist!

By the power of God, Ezekiel spoke,
and the dry bones in the valley
all awoke!

The bones came together and
God added flesh!
But they could not truly live
until God added His breath!

What are the Dry Bones in your
life today?
Does poverty, sickness,
depression and doubt get
in your way?

Does your soul feel fragmented
and scattered about?
Call on the Bone Collector
He will help you work it out!

Just as He breathed new life into
dry bones, He can do the same
for you! God is your Bone Collector,
He's waiting to give you the breath
that will make your life brand new!

Ezekiel 37:1-14

DRY PLACE

A dry place is a place where
things never seem to change!
No matter how hard you try your
life issues remain the same!

God, who loves you, will sometimes
leave you in this dry place!
He does this because He wants you
to seek His face!

There will come a sign, a sound
and then a storm!
Don't be concerned, for God is
standing by and will not let you
suffer any harm!

Watch for a sign that whatever the
issue is it can be fixed!
The devil meant it for harm, he forgot
that God would get in the mix!

Listen for a sound, a sound from
above! Reminding you that God
has promised His unconditional love!

Know that a storm will come, but
you need not fear!
There is a blessing in each storm,
so don't be afraid God is standing near!

Were it not for the storm some of us
would never pray!
It's in the storm that we meet Jesus,
He will offer shelter, and show you the way!

We all must go through something to
be able to testify!
So, look for a sign, listen for a sound,
stand up to the storm, and the place you
are in will no longer be dry!

Ezekiel 37:4-6

GATE CALLED BEAUTIFUL

Stuck at a gate called Beautiful and everyone passing
you by. Stuck at a gate called Beautiful and just can't
understand why.

Sitting in a situation because it's all you know. Praying
for someone to pass by and show you the way to go.

Stuck at a gate called Beautiful so close you can see the
other side! Hand stretched out and begging "someone
please come be my guide!"

Stuck at a gate called Beautiful, good times running
into bad. Wishing you could find your way back to
the peace you once had.

Stuck at a gate called Beautiful, stuck with the
audacity of hope! A hope in the name of "Jesus"
by which all curses can be broke!

Thank God for that gate called Beautiful, Jesus
will meet you there! He will put an end to your
struggles and relieve you of all your cares!

Acts 3:1-10

HOLY SPIRIT

Holy Spirit come sit with me! Please
sit and hold my hand! I need for You
to comfort me and help me understand!

One day they were here, the next they were
gone! Tell me Holy Spirit how do I go on?

Someone I love has been taken away!
I prayed so hard, I wanted them to stay!

I thank God for the memories that we shared!
I pray that through my actions they knew how
much I cared!

Holy Spirit come sit with me! Hold me in Your
arms and help me find peace!

Close the door let no one else in! Help me
Holy Spirit! Ease this pain within!

My heart feels such grief! Yet in my spirit
I see, that their body was just a shell, and
now their spirit is set free!

Free from this world, free from sickness and
pain! Free to walk with Jesus! My grief is
their gain!

Holy Spirit come sit with me! Please! Sit
and hold my hand! I need for You to comfort
me and help me understand!

LOOK UP!

How do you let go of a loved one when their
time on earth is done? When your heart is heavy
and burdened, how do you let go of your loved one?

Know that they have returned to their Heavenly
Father and are now safe in His loving arms. Safe from
all danger, safe from all harm.

I pray that in time you will be able to look up and wipe
the tears from your eyes. Look up and see a new star
twinkling in the sky!

New colors have been added to God's rainbow! A sweet
spirit set free to fly. Their bodies will soon fade away but
their spirit will never die.

So look up and see your loved one, they are smiling down
at you, and wanting you to know they will see you in Heaven
and that they loved you too!

Look up!

NIGHT LIGHT

When I rise in the morning,
before the sun shows it's face.
I see a beautiful moon, hanging
with such majesty and grace.

Illuminate the sky,
that the moon doesn't do!
It hangs through the darkness
as a sign for me and you!

A sign that God is with us
through the darkness of night!
He is watching over us and
will soon give us light!

Genesis 1:14-17

WELCOME HOME!

I can only imagine the day that I
see Your face! I can only imagine
spending eternity in that heavenly place!

I can only imagine walking down those
streets of gold! To once again see my loved
ones and Your face Father to finally behold!

I can only imagine how awesome it will be,
when You call my name, when my spirit is set free!

Free to worship and give You praise! To walk
around heaven with holy hands always raised!

I can only imagine standing before Your throne!
Hearing Your voice as You say, "Well done my
child, welcome home!"

Psalm 86:10-12

Higgins
Publishing

CONTACT THE AUTHOR
FOR BOOK SIGNINGS AND
SPEAKING ENGAGEMENTS FOR
SPECIAL EVENTS AT:
PHONE: 510-303-7769

~

SUBMIT REVIEWS ONLINE
AT: WWW.AMAZON.COM